FINE ARTS AS THERAPY

Plato's Teaching Organized and Discussed

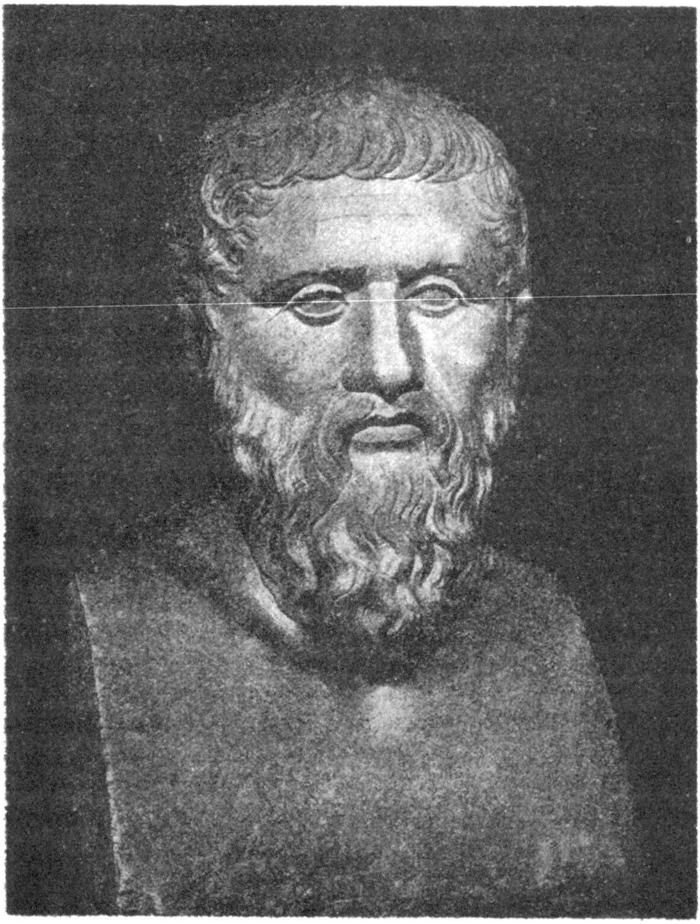

PLATO

(427-346 B.C.)

FINE ARTS AS THERAPY

Plato's Teaching Organized and Discussed

By

CONSTANTINE CAVARNOS

INSTITUTE FOR BYZANTINE
AND MODERN GREEK STUDIES
115 Gilbert Road
Belmont, Massachusetts 02178-2200
U.S.A.

Design and Typesetting by:
E. Marshall Publishing & Translation Services
Brookline, Massachusetts 02146

Published by THE INSTITUTE FOR BYZANTINE
AND MODERN GREEK STUDIES, INC.
115 Gilbert Road, Belmont, Massachusetts 02178-2200, U.S.A.

Printed in the United States of America

Library of Congress Catalog Card Number: 98-70118

Clothbound ISBN: 1-884729-32-0
Paperbound ISBN: 1-884729-33-9

FOREWORD

Fine Arts as Therapy appears for the first time in book form. Dr. Cavarnos traces the historical origins in Plato's teachings and gives both the health specialist and the general reader the Western point of view that human expression which is organized to produce a response of aesthetic pleasure can simultaneously contribute to healing. Consequently the use of this therapeutic modality is ultimately the responsibility of the patient, either through performance participation or through witness. This point of view stands in stark contrast to the 20th century practice of dependency upon medicines or groups.

Drawing especially from Plato's *Republic* and *Laws*, Dr. Cavarnos clarifies Plato's view of the "whole man," as a structure of psyche or soul which is expressed through the body, pointing out that both the psyche and body must be involved in therapy in order to effect a cure. Plato makes distinctions between the conscious and unconscious states of cognitive and emotional centers.

In the second part of this book Dr. Cavarnos explains Plato's definition of health and disease of the psyche and the body as they are related to harmony, proportion, courage, and love.

In the third part Dr. Cavarnos points out Plato's view that the fine arts must be assimilated and developed through the medium of "true education." Plato uses the term "techne" and not "fine art," which includes music, painting, sculpture, literature, science, and philosophy. Emphasis is put on skill and method of creation, performance, and communication.

Dr. Cavarnos explains Plato's distinction between "true art" and "pseudo art" in the fourth section. "True art" is seen as fostering the health of both the body and the soul.

The subject of assimilation of the good and bad, as well as purification by true catharsis is related to beauty, and to modern psychoanalysis which is covered in the fifth section.

Plato's view of art as therapy, especially as it relates to philosophy, literature, comedy, rhetoric, music, dance, and the other arts is illuminated in the sixth section. In the concluding section Plato's view of the prevention and therapy of disease is related to his standpoint regarding the use of medicines and surgery. Dr. Cavarnos then traces Plato's connection to Asklepios and to Pythagoras.

This book gives an invaluable historical perspective for so many current points of view in medicine, psychiatry, and the arts.

XENIA LUCAS
Associate Professor, Director of the
Graduate Program in Art and Psychiatry

Boston University
January, 1998

PREFACE

This brief treatise was first delivered as a lecture at Boston University on March 12, 1975, before the students of Professor Xenia Lucas' graduate seminar "Art as Therapy." The lecture was delivered there again in the years 1976 and 1977.

In 1977, the Academy of Athens published it in its Yearbook *Philosophia*, a journal prepared by its Research Center for Greek Philosophy. In publishing it, the Center at the end added a Greek Summary written by Dr. Myrto Dragona-Monachou, a member of the Editorial Board.

On April 9, 1981, the lecture was presented at Boston University at an International Congress of Psychotherapy of Expression. The Congress was organized by Irene Jakab, M.D., Ph.D., Chairman, and Xenia Lucas, Co-chairman, and was sponsored by the American Society of Psychopathology of Expression and Boston University. The Society published it in 1981 in its journal, *The Personality of the Therapist*, edited by Dr. Irene Jakab.

The complete lecture appears now for the first time in book form, with the addition of the Greek Summary at the end (for those Greek readers who are not fluent in English and as an aid for others who know Greek), and with improvements in expression, corrections in some of the footnotes, and additions to the documentation. In order to make it easier for the reader to follow the course of the discussion, I have divided the text into seven chapters.

This work is addressed to all persons who are interested in philosophy, the fine arts, the medical art, and the restoration and preservation of mental and physical health.

CONSTANTINE CAVARNOS

Belmont, Massachusetts
January 1998

CONTENTS

1

INTRODUCTORY

In this lecture, I shall discuss what the great Athenian philosopher Plato says about the role the fine arts can play in the therapy of diseases, and more broadly in the improvement of the condition of both the psyche and the body. His teaching on this subject is rich and very valuable. However, it is not presented systematically in some one of his works, but is scattered in many of them. In almost every one of his dialogues there is something pertinent to this subject. Those which are richest in such teaching are the *Republic* and the *Laws*. Hence, I shall draw a great deal more from these dialogues than from his other works. I shall not rely on secondary sources, on what others have said about Plato's teaching on this subject. The reason for this is that no one, to my knowledge, has dealt with this part of Plato's philosophy to any significant extent: I know of no book or even article on the subject.

Since our concern is with the therapy of man, especially of the psyche, and of the body through the psyche, it is necessary at the outset to have an adequate idea of man as Plato conceives him, particularly of the psyche or soul. According to Plato, *man is a psyche using a body as an instrument.*[1] Like many philosophers since his time, such as Plotinos, Descartes, Locke and Bergson, he believes that the psyche and the body *interact*: the psyche acts on the body, and the body acts on the psyche.[2] Therefore, if one of these is in a good state, its influence on the other will be good, while if it is in a bad state, its influence will be bad. Negative states of the psyche are reflected in the body, result

---

[1] Thus, the soul uses the bodily senses, especially sight and hearing, in enquiry about the physical world (*Phaedo* 79c). See my book *Plato's View of Man*, Belmont, MA, 1975, pp. 56-64.

[2] See e.g. *Phaedo* 81a-d, 83d, and *Plato's View of man*, pp. 69-71.

in bodily disorders, and conversely, bad states of the body result in disorderly mental states.

It follows, that therapy, whether it aims at correcting a state of the psyche or a state of the body, must take into account the *whole* human being. Therapy must approach the state both from the side of the psyche and from the side of the body, and, moreover, of the *whole* psyche and the *whole* body, *beginning* with the *psyche*. In the dialogue *Charmides*, Plato puts forth the view that "as you ought not to attempt to cure the eyes without the head, or the head without the body, so neither ought you to attempt to cure the body without the soul. And this is the reason why the cure of many diseases is unknown to the physicians of Hellas, because they are ignorant of the whole, which ought to be studied also; for the part can never be well unless the whole is well." And then he adds: "For all good and evil in the body and in the whole man originates in the soul, and overflows from thence, as if from the head into the eyes. And therefore if the head and body are to be well, you must begin by curing the soul; that is the first thing."[3]

Plato emphasizes that of the two terms of the psyche-body relationship, *primacy* belongs to the *psyche*. By nature, it is proper for the psyche to rule and the body to be ruled.[4] The soul is dynamic, creative: it is *originative* of motion, of change, whereas the body does not originate motion or change, but only communicates it. Hence, in the last analysis, the condition of the body is a result of the condition of the psyche.

The body is rendered *alive* by the psyche. More than this, the body is *formed* by the psyche. The psyche makes the body as a weaver makes a cloak; with this difference, that the activity of the psyche continues uninterruptedly throughout life. The body, says Plato in the *Phaedo*, "is constantly changing and being destroyed, while man still lives, and the soul is always weaving anew that which wears

---

[3] *Charmides*, 156-157. Cf. *Republic* III. 403d.

[4] *Phaedo* 79e-80a, 94b-e; *Laws* X. 896b-c.

out."[5] In the language of modern physiology, a process of catabolism is constantly taking place in the body, and this is counteracted unceasingly by the reverse process of anabolism. According to Plato, the process of anabolism is directed by the psyche. The figure of the weaver and the cloak brings to mind Shakespeare's remark that "sleep knits up the raveled sleeve of care."[6] Plato would have commented on this passage of Shakespeare that sleep is not an entity which exercises causal efficacy, but is only a relatively inactive state of the body, during which the psyche intensifies its efforts to reknit the parts of the 'garment' that have been raveled by the cares of waking life.

Implicit in the view that the psyche forms and repairs the body is the idea that there is an *un*conscious level of the psyche, which directs the anabolic processes; for we are not conscious of doing so. The belief that the unconscious is a recent

---

[5] *Phaedo* 87d-e; cf. 91d.

[6] *Macbeth* II, ii.

discovery of psychology, particularly of psychoanalysis, is wrong. The idea of the unconscious is at least as old as Plato's philosophy, being a fundamental part of his theory of man and of his theory of knowledge.[7]

In some of his works, Plato makes certain statements that have been taken by some to imply that he regarded the body as *inherently* evil. He has been viewed, in other words, as a forerunner of *Manichaeism.* Now Plato speaks in a few places of the body as a '*tomb*' (*séma*) of the soul,[8] or as a '*prison*' (*heirgmós*) of the soul.[9] But these statements do *not* justify us in taking Plato to mean that the body is *intrinsically* bad. We have his own explicit assertion that "the body is neither good nor evil," as well as his already quoted statement that

---

[7] See my books *Plato's View of Man*, p. 28, and *The Classical Theory of Relations*, 1975, pp. 30, 36.

[8] *Cratylus* 400e; *Phaedrus* 250c; *Gorgias* 493a.

[9] *Phaedo* 81d-e, 82e, 83d; cf. *Cratylus* 400, *Phaedrus* 250c.

"all good and evil originates in the *soul*."[10] As to the body being a 'tomb' or a 'prison' of the soul, Plato explains that in the final analysis it is the psyche which renders the body such, through lack of vigilance, through ignorance, through intemperance of one form or another."[11] This is a topic that requires considerable discussion, and we shall return to it. The whole subject of physical disease, its causes, prevention and treatment, is linked with it.

Since man is a psyche and the body is only an instrument of the psyche, it is necessary to discuss the structure of the psyche, when it is such as it ought to be, or 'according to nature,' and then to view the psyche when this order is disrupted, when the condition of the psyche is 'contrary to nature.' Plato teaches that the human psyche has three distinguishable parts or powers. These are the *rational*, the *spirited*, and the *appetitive*. The rational part is the highest, the appetitive the lowest,

---

[10] *Lysis*, 217a, *Charmides* 156a; cf. *Republic* III. 409c.

[11] See e.g. *Phaedo* 82e-83a.

and the spirited intermediate. This is the natural hierarchical order. Each of these parts or powers is in turn distinguishable into a cognitive and an emotional element. The rational power consists of intellect (*nóesis*) and love (*éros*); the spirited, of opinion or conviction (*pístis*) and spirit (*thymós*); and the appetitive, of conjecture (*eikasía*) and desire (*epithymía*). The rational power is directed to the true, the good, and the beautiful; the spirited, to ruling, conquering and getting honors; the appetitive, to the satisfaction of the desires for food, drink, comfort, and reproduction, and to material gain, because such desires are generally satisfied by the help of money. The rational and the appetitive powers are opposed principles. In the man who is striving for self-development, the rational part fights against and restrains the appetitive power in its tendency to excess. In the struggle between reason and desire, the spirited part, which is characterized by the feelings of anger, indignation and confidence, usually sides with reason, and never takes part with desire against reason. Thus, when a man's desires violently prevail over his reason, the spirited principle is on the side of reason: the man is angry, reviles himself. Also, the spirited element stirs us up to indignation when we see the just trampled under foot by the unjust. But if it is not controlled by the rational element, the spirited power leads us to reckless boldness and self-assertion.[12]

When the proper hierarchy is preserved within the psyche, when the rational power is developed and rules the non-rational powers—the spirited and the appetitive—and these obey the commands of reason, so that each part of the psyche carries on rightly its own distinctive functions, the state of the psyche is one of harmony, health.

This state of harmony or health is regulated and maintained by the *four main excellences or virtues*: wisdom, courage, temperance, and justice. *Wisdom* (*sophía*, *phrónesis*) is the virtue that pertains to the rational power. It is, in the first place, *self-*

---

[12] For a fuller discussion of the three powers of the soul, see my *Plato's View of Man*, pp. 31-39.

knowledge, that is, knowledge of man's true nature and destiny, and of the necessary means for fulfilling it. Wisdom is the profound realization that each of us is essentially not a body, but a soul, which is far superior to the body in worth and immortal, and hence deserving the greatest attention and care. Wisdom is also a keen awareness of the fact that the body is an instrument of the soul, an instrument which the soul should make proper use of and keep in good condition, so that it will be an efficient instrument and not a hindrance. Thus, wisdom embraces knowledge of *human nature and destiny*, and knowledge of the true *values* that pertain to human nature and destiny, directing us to the right use of our psyche and body and of everything pertaining to them.

With regard to values, it should be explained that Plato distinguishes two categories, which he calls 'divine goods' (*agathá theía*) and 'human goods' (*agathá anthrópina*). The first class of goods are superior to the second. Divine goods are absolute, whereas human goods are conditional.

Among the divine goods are the four main virtues that have already been mentioned: wisdom, temperance, justice, and courage. Among the human goods are bodily health, beauty and strength, and a sufficiency of material resources. The goods of each of these categories form a scale, some being higher than others. The order in which they have been mentioned is the order of their value. Thus, wisdom is the highest of the divine goods, and physical health is the highest of human goods. Plato assigns supreme value to wisdom. He does so because wisdom is the excellence of the highest faculty of man, which rules the other powers; and because it is the guiding principle in the formation of the other virtues and in the acquisition of the human goods. The latter are called conditional, in that they are good *if* they are *rightly* used, and their right use depends on the possession of the divine goods, i.e., of the four excellences of the psyche.[13]

---

[13] *Laws* I. 631b-c, II. 661a, III. 688b; cf. *Euthydemus* 281a-282, 288e-289a, *Phaedo* 69b, *Republic* IX. 591c-d.

To the spirited power, which comes next after the rational in the hierarchical structure of the psyche, belongs the excellence of *courage* (*andreía*). This virtue consists in obedience of the spirited power in pleasure and pain to the commands of reason. Courage involves right opinion or conviction as to what is to be feared and what is not to be feared.

Temperance (*sophrosyne*) belongs to all three parts of the psyche. It exists when the spirited and the appetitive powers agree that the highest faculty, reason, ought to rule and they should obey. In other words, temperance is proper subordination, the submission of the lower parts of the soul to the highest without coercion. Further, it is the observance of measure or moderation in the exercise of each of these powers.

The fourth main virtue, *justice* (*dikaiosyne*), similarly belongs to all three parts of the psyche. Viewed as an inward quality, justice is the harmonious working together of all three parts, where each does its own peculiar work and does not take over functions proper to the other parts. It is the quality which preserves these. That is, justice can be looked at both as an effect and as a cause.

After defining the four main virtues in the *Republic*, Plato remarks that it is obvious that virtue is the *health*, *beauty*, and *vigor* of the *soul*.[14]

When the hierarchical structure of the soul is disrupted, when the natural order is inverted, there result *disease*, *ugliness*, and *weakness* of the *soul*. This inversion (*anatropé*)[15] can be of greater or lesser seriousness. One form of inversion is when the rule of the rational faculty is replaced by the rule of the spirited element. The striving for honors and power replaces the love of wisdom and understanding, the love of the good and beautiful. Life is now guided by custom and the letter of the law, unillumined by rational insight and wisdom.

A more serious inversion of the hierarchical structure of the psyche takes place when not only

---

14 *Republic* IV. 444d-e.

15 On the notion of inversion, see esp. *Republic* IV. 442b and *Gorgias* 481c.

reason, but also the spirited element are pushed aside, and the appetitive element takes over the leadership of the soul. In this case, the rational and the spirited part of the soul are forced to act as slaves of the appetitive. Reason has now to calculate and consider nothing but ways of gratifying the sensuous desires and of getting more and more money, while the spirited power has to admire and honor nothing but riches and rich men.[16]

This, however, is not the worst form of inversion or disorder that can take place in the psyche. The complete turning upside down of the true order of the psyche occurs when some *lawless* (*paránomos*) desire becomes enthroned as the ruler within the soul. For within the appetitive power there are *three levels of desires*, and the condition of the soul is worst when the lowest desires tyrannize over the whole soul. There are, Plato notes, *necessary desires* and *unnecessary desires*; and among the unnecessary desires there are some that

---

[16] *Republic* VIII. 553c-d.

are lawless.[17] The *necessary* desires, such as the desire for food, have to be satisfied, for the proper maintenance of the health and strength of the body. Their satisfaction is bad only when it is immoderate, or when one seeks, for example, dainties instead of simple, wholesome food. The desire for dainties and that for luxuries are examples of *unnecessary desires*. *Lawless* desires are those unnecessary desires which are forbidden by the laws of well-governed states and by the highest principle in man, reason. Examples of lawless desires cited by Plato are the desire for murder, for incest, for adultery, for homosexual relations.[18] He remarks that it seems likely that lawless desires are present in all, manifesting themselves in sleep.[19] In some persons, he says, such desires are controlled, and are either banished or become few and weak, whereas in others no effort is made to control and eradicate

---

[17] *Ibid.* 559d-661a, IX. 571a-572b.

[18] *Republic* V. 461, IX. 571c-d, 574d-e; *Laws* I. 636c, VIII. 841-842a.

[19] *Republic* IX. 571b, 572b.

them, and hence unlawful desires are many and strong. In the latter class of individuals, one such desire in time becomes the ruling force. It is nourished into greatness by the idle, spendthrift desires, until it breaks out in frenzy. A man in whom this takes places becomes, says Plato, "for his waking life the man he used to be from time to time in his *dreams*, ready to shed blood or do any dreadful deed."[20]

In a soul in which there is a turning of its hierarchical structure upside down, instead of the excellence of wisdom there is the vice of *ignorance*; instead of courage, *cowardice*; instead of temperance, *intemperance*; instance of justice, *injustice*. Seen from the ethical standpoint, such a psyche is *bad*; seen from the aesthetic standpoint, deformed, *ugly*; seen from the medical point of view, *sick*. And as psyche and body act upon one another, the body is adversely affected.

---

[20] *Republic* 572e; *Laws* VIII. 836c-839a, 841b.

In connection with the medical viewpoint, it should be noted that Plato characterizes each the vices (*kakíai*) or negative qualities just mentioned as a *disease* (*nósos*) of the soul. He calls ignorance a disease of the soul, and applies the same term to intemperance, injustice, and cowardice.[21] It must also be noted that the examples which Plato presents of men suffering from these maladies do not conform, except in certain respects, to the definitions or descriptions of either schizophrenia or paranoia given in modern medical books. The term *schizophrenia*, which is Greek, does not appear in his writings, while the word *paránoia* appears only three times.[22] The latter means, etymologically, "being beside (*pará*) or out of one's mind (*nous*)." Plato uses the term paranoia to denote madness or insanity in general. He prefers to denote insanity by the cognate term *ánoia*, which means absence of mind, of reason, and is usually translated as 'folly,' and by the term *manía*, 'madness.' *Anoia* is for him a broader term than mania, embracing unconscious

---

[21] *Republic* X. 609a-e; *Timaeus* 86b, 88b; *Sophist* 228d.

[22] *Phaedrus* 266a; *Laws* XI. 928e, 929d.

ignorance or stupidity (*amathía*)[23] and 'madness' (*manía*).[24] Probably such extreme cases of psychic disorders as are denoted by our terms schizophrenia and paranoia were quite rare if not altogether unknown in ancient Greece. The closest Plato comes to describing a case of schizophrenia is in his discussions of the tyrannical man, the dictator, and of the incontinent man. The tyrannical man also presents features of paranoia: he is described in the *Republic* as being beset with fear, full of convulsions and pains, and compelled to pass his life fighting and combating with other men.[25] Incontinence is described in the *Timaeus* as a form of madness (*manía*) that consists in an inability to control the reproductive function. It results in excessive pleasures and pains, which render the rational faculty inoperative as a power of guidance and control, for the most part of one's life. The Athenian philosopher remarks that when a man is overjoyed, or contrariwise suffers excessively from

---

[23] *Timaeus* 86b-d.

[24] *Ibid.*

[25] *Republic* IX. 579d-e.

pain, "he is unable either to see or to hear anything correctly, and he is at such a time distraught and wholly incapable of exercising reason."[26] Such madness, according to Plato, has as its proximate cause a bad bodily state. There is an overproduction of seed, which causes intense lust. This bodily state is in turn a result of wrong education and wrong mode of life."[27]

It is necessary to explain that our philosopher does not regard all forms of 'madness' as pathological. There are for him four types of 'madness' which are not bad, but good, *non-pathological*, having a divine origin and being releases from customary habits,[28] modes of rising above the restrictions of discussive reason, of logic. He discusses four kinds of non-pathological madness. One of them is the madness of *prophecy* (*mantiké*); another is the mystic (*telestiké*); a third is the *poetic* (*poietiké*), or what we call poetic 'inspiration;' and

---

[26] *Timaeus* 86c; cf. *Republic* III. 402e.

[27] *Timaeus* 86e; cf. *Phaedrus* 265a, *Laws* VIII. 839b-841c.

[28] *Phaedrus* 265a.

the fourth is the madness of *love* (*éros*). These four kinds of madness are viewed as higher states, as *supranormal* phenomena. This is especially true of the last mentioned form of 'madness,' that of love, which Plato regards as the *highest*, *best* kind of madness.[29] Love, as understood by Plato, is love of the beautiful viewed as good.[30] It has various manifestations, some higher than others. Its highest form is the love of ideals, such as wisdom, temperance, justice, holiness, love of the divine. This love is best seen in the philosopher, Plato believes, for the true philosopher, despising earthly riches and honors, as well as the customary enjoyments, is absorbed with the quest of higher values, of higher truth, of the supreme Good, of God.[31]

Plato's concern is clearly not with the therapy of these good forms of 'madness,' but with the treatment of states that he regards as really

---

[29] *Ibid.* 244-250a, 265b.

[30] *Ibid.* 246d-250e; *Symposium* 204b-205d; *Republic* III. 403a.

[31] *Phaedrus* 248e; *Republic* VI. 500b-c.

pathological. One such state, as we have already seen, is ignorance. He calls ignorance the greatest of the diseases of the soul.[32] It is the greatest, because it is the root cause of other diseases of the soul. Of ignorance, there are two kinds: conscious ignorance (*ágnoia*) and unconscious ignorance (*amathía*). Conscious ignorance is ignorance that knows it does not know. Unconscious ignorance is ignorance that believes itself to be knowledge; it is what is sometimes termed 'stupidity.' Such ignorance is far worse than conscious ignorance, because it blocks the way to progress in knowledge and understanding. One who is in a state of unconscious ignorance with respect to a particular subject has the delusion that he possesses the knowledge which he lacks, and hence makes no effort to acquire it. Other states of the psyche which Plato regards as pathological and hence in need of therapy are, as we have already seen: intemperance, injustice, and cowardice.

---

[32] *Timaeus* 86b.

2

HEALTH AND DISEASE ANALYZED

I have spoken of various pathological states or diseases. But *what* is *disease*? To understand what disease is, one must understand what *health* is, health being something positive and disease something negative, a privation of health. Plato analyzes health in *aesthetic* terms. Health is *harmony, order, proportion, rhythm*. Disease is the *absence* or *negation* of these, as we have seen in the discussion of the inversion of the hierarchical structure of the psyche: it is *dis*harmony, *dis*order, *dis*proportion, *lack* of rhythm. This holds for diseases of the body as well as those of the soul. The body is healthy when it contains various substances in the right proportion, neither to excess nor deficiently;[33] when its functions or 'movements,' as Plato calls them, are harmoniously interrelated; and when it is harmoniously related to the psyche.[34] In the case of the psyche, the virtues which constitute its health are forms of harmony.[35] Thus, wisdom is in part an apprehension and reflection within the intellect of the objective cosmic order, and of the perfection and beauty of the realm of archetypes, forms or ideas.[36] Courage is the harmony between the spirited and the rational powers of the psyche, the latter counseling what is to be feared and the former obeying. Temperance involves the harmonious relationship between all three parts of the psyche, the rational part ruling and the spirited and appetitive parts obeying without the need of coercion. It is also the observation of measure, proportion, in the exercise of each part of

---

[33] *Phaedo* 93a; *Symposium* 188a ff.; *Republic* X. 609; *Laws* X. 906c.

[34] *Timaeus* 87d-e.

[35] *Phaedo* 93e; *Republic* III. 410e-411a, IV. 430e.

[36] *Republic* VI. 508; *Plato's View of Man*, pp. 20-21.

the psyche. And justice is the harmonious functioning of the three parts of the psyche, each doing its own work and not interfering with the work of the other parts.

3

EDUCATION AND THE FINE ARTS

We come now to the problem of therapy (*therapeía*) of the psyche and the body, and the question of the role the fine arts can play in therapy. In order to explain how they can be used to this end, it is necessary to add to what I have said thus far a brief account of Plato's theory of true education (*orthé paideía*), because the fine arts are viewed by him as *parts* of such education. Now education is for him an enterprise that is unsurpassed by any other in importance.[37] It has two major divisions. One of these is 'music' (*mousiké*), the other is 'gymnastic' (*gymnastiké*).[38] The term '*music*' is derived from the '*Muses*,' whom the Greeks

---

[37] *Phaedrus* 241c; *Republic* III. 416c, IV, 423d-e.

[38] *Gorgias* 264b-c; *Cratylus* 50d; *Republic* II. 376e; *Crito* 50d-e.

imagined as the 'goddesses' of the arts and sciences. The division of education which Plato calls 'music' embraces not only what is ordinarily called music,[39] but also the rest of the fine arts and in addition mathematics (arithmetic, plane and solid geometry), astronomy, harmonics, the correlation of the sciences, and philosophy, which according to him is the supreme branch of knowledge.[40] The term 'fine art' does not appear in Plato's writings. He uses simply the term 'art' (*téchne*) to denote what we call the 'fine arts'—e.g., music, painting, sculpture, literature—and in addition the various 'useful arts' and branches of knowledge. The sciences are arts in the sense that they are not only specific systems of *knowledge* but are also certain *skills*, involving a *method* of investigation and of expression or communication.[41] Philosophy itself is in this sense an art.[42] For our purposes, we may distinguish the

---

39 *Gorgias* 449d; *Phaedo* 61a.

40 *Phaedo* 61; *Republic* VIII. 533c-534e.

41 *Republic* I. 346 ff., VI. 511c; *Phaedo* 97b, 99E-100a.

42 *Republic* VII. 532c-533e.

fine arts from the arts in general by saying that the fine arts are concerned with *making*, and more narrowly with making works that are expressive of *beauty*.

The division of education called 'music' in the wide sense of the term is concerned with the *soul*, with its care, harmonious development and purification from every defect or evil. It seeks not only to *develop* properly the *potentialities* of the soul, but also to *prevent disorders* or defects from arising in it, and to *correct* any that may be present.

'*Gymnastic*,' the other major division of education, has to do with the *body*. It is divided into two parts: regimen and physical exercises. The Greek word for regimen is *díaita*, from which is derived the English word 'diet.' *Regimen* is a prescribed manner of life based on knowledge of the principles of hygiene, of the whole science of preventive medicine. It pertains to the quality and quantity of food and drink, and the time when one should partake of them, as well as to the nature and duration of rest, habituation to hardships, and so on.[43] Physical exercises (*gymnásia*) are movements that are particularly valuable for building a healthy, strong, agile, and beautiful body.[44] Among the forms of exercise which he cites are the dance, walking, running, and wrestling.[45] Thus, the dance is set apart from all the other fine arts by being placed under the heading of gymnastic, of education that pertains to the body. However, Plato points out that true gymnastic aims at improving not only the body, but also, and chiefly, the psyche.[46] Gymnastic strengthens the spirited element up to a point, helping develop courage, weakens lust, and fosters the development of temperance. Exercises that have the opposite effects are ruled out. Thus, those that tend to overdevelop the muscles, and to strengthen the spirited element to the point of ferocity, are

---

43 *Ibid.* III. 403a ff.; *Protagoras* 313-314; *Laws* XII. 942d.

44 *Gorgias* 452b, 465b; *Republic* III. 410b ff.

45 VII. 795e-796, VIII. 832d ff.; *Laws* VII. 789c-d.

46 *Republic* III. 410c; *Laws* VII. 791c.

asserted to be vulgar and unworthy of being called *paideia*.[47]

Studies of a purely utilitarian nature, concerned with man's material needs and in general with man's biological survival—various trades, agriculture, mining, and other ways of earning money—are not included in the first division of education.[48] The arts and sciences which are included by Plato in his curriculum designed for an ideal State are all what we call 'liberal.' They are such as tend to improve the soul, although some of them—for instance, mathematics and astronomy—happen to have also utilitarian value. Arithmetic, for example, is useful for everyday dealings, but its main value as a part of education lies in fact that it is good intellectual discipline, helps develop the faculty of reason, trains us to think, draws the mind towards the abstract, the true, the eternal, and thus prepares one for philosophy. The same is true of geometry.[49]

---

[47] *Republic* III. 410b ff.

[48] *Euthydemus* 288e-289a.

[49] *Republic* VII. 525c-527e; *Laws* V. 747b.

Astronomy and harmonics serve the same purpose, and further initiate us into higher truth and reality, bringing to our attention what is *beautiful*: the first the harmony of the motions of the heavenly bodies, the second the harmony of sounds.[50] The study of the correlation of all these sciences, or what we would call the 'philosophy of science,' further brings to our attention the beautiful and the good, by showing the harmony of one branch of knowledge with another.[51] All these sciences: arithmetic, geometry, harmonics, and the correlation of them, prepare the mind for the study of the highest art and science: 'dialectic' or philosophy.[52] The supreme object of philosophy, as conceived by Plato, is the discovery and contemplation of the highest Good, which he terms the 'Idea of good,' a reality that is absolute, suprasensible, eternal. This Good, viewed from the detached, aesthetic standpoint, is an object

50 *Republic* VII. 530-531.

51 *Ibid.* 531.

52 *Ibid.* 532a-533e.

of inexpressible Beauty. The contemplation of it constitutes the highest fulfillment of spiritual eros.[53]

---

[53] *Republic* VI. 505a-509b, VII. 517b-c, 526d-e. Cf. my book *Plato's Theory of Fine Art*, Athens, 1973, pp. 26-27. The 'Idea of Good' has been identified by many Platonic scholars with God.

4

TRUE ART AND PSEUDO ART

To properly understand Plato's teaching on fine art as a means of therapy one must be aware of one further element in his philosophy: his sharp distinction between *true* art and *pseudo* art. True art is governed by the principles of *idealism*, *rationality*, *simplicity*, *clarity*, *organic unity*, *appropriateness*, *measure*, *proportion*, *harmony*, *rhythm*. It is guided by wisdom, that is, by knowledge of man's true nature and ultimate aim in life, by knowledge of the Divine and man's proper relation to it, and by a clear apprehension of the true hierarchy of values that should be the object of man's aspiration. Such art seeks to convey this wisdom and to help mold character consonant with it. True art springs from man's highest faculty, the rational. It seeks to nourish and to develop this by means of such knowledge; and, by embodying the principles that have just been listed, to bring the other powers of the psyche into harmony with the rational power.

Pseudo art, on the other hand, is not guided by wisdom, but is directed by personal or public opinion, by conjecture or imagination, and gives expression to wrong forms of character and action. Pseudo art presents what is ugly as though it were beautiful, disease as if it were health; and it praises evil under the guise of good. Thus it has the effect of suggesting, and hence inclining people to do, what is ugly instead of what is beautiful. And it results in their developing various forms of ugliness or disorder of the soul and thereby of the body. Pseudo art addresses itself not to the highest part of the psyche, but to the lower parts. It strengthens these, weakens the intellectual power, and thus leads to the disruption of the hierarchical structure of the psyche.[54]

---

[54] For a fuller discussion of the distinction between true art and pseudo art see *Plato's Theory of Fine Art*, pp. 13-22, 26, 64-80.

It is clear that for Plato *not all* the creations of what are called the fine arts have therapeutic value, but only works of *true* art. Works of pseudo art do not have such value; they are either indifferent or positively harmful, implanting disharmony and disorder in the soul, or augmenting the disharmony and discord already present in it. I am speaking here of *works* of art when used to act upon a patient. I am *not* speaking of the effect of the *process* of artistic creation *by* a patient who is himself engaged in such a process—painting, for instance, or singing, regardless of his competence. Plato does not discuss this, except incidentally. Thus, he tells us that while Socrates was in prison, before his death, he composed poetry, something he had never done in the past. In particular, he composed a hymn to Apollo and metrical versions of some of Aesop's fables. Socrates is reported in *Phaedo* 60e to have said that he did this because often in his past life he had a dream in which he was told: "Socrates, make music and work at it." By composing this poetry, he wanted to make sure that he was not neglecting an activity that was divinely enjoined upon him. Artistic activity is viewed here as a means of easing one's conscience, effecting a harmony between oneself and the Divine.

In their true form, the fine arts constitute an important kind of education. Their aim, like that of the rest of education, is the harmonious development of man, the promotion of health of body and soul. They are intended both as ways of *preventing* diseases or deformations of soul and body, of *remedying* those that have arisen, and also of developing man's higher potentialities.

The fact that the fine arts are viewed as parts of education does not necessarily mean that one must be exposed to them in a *formal* manner, as in classrooms. For Plato and the ancient Greeks in general the term *paideia*, 'education,' has a narrower meaning, denoting formal education, and a broader meaning, denoting both formal education and all other cultural influences. All such influences, at every stage of life, were viewed as constituting *paideia*. Taken in the sense of all such influences, *paideia* commences at childhood and continues throughout one's life. As envisaged by Plato, fine arts such as architecture, painting, and sculpture exert educational influences from their own proper setting in the community, as parts of the surroundings in which one is brought up and lives. Other arts, such as literature and music, act both by being presented formally, by a teacher, and by being presented informally on various occasions of life.

Fine arts act upon the psyche in a beneficent manner by *conveying ideals*, such as the virtues that we noted earlier. Plato speaks of the fine arts as 'imitating' ideals. "Imitating' is to be taken to mean *expressing*, *conveying*, *symbolizing* or *pointing to* such ideals *vividly* and hence effectively. The rational faculty by nature apprehends these ideals; and the repeated apprehension of them, especially during what are called the formative years, definitely effects the formation of human character (*ethos*) in the likeness of these ideals.

5

ASSIMILATION AND PURIFICATION IN THERAPY

Plato enunciates a very important psychological and pedagogical principle relevant to the action of the arts: that *one becomes like that which he habitually contemplates*. He states this principle in the *Republic* as follows: A man cannot help imitating (*mimésthai*) that with which he holds converse (*homileí*) with admiration.[55] To this statement he adds: "The philosopher, holding converse with the divine and orderly, becomes divine and orderly, as far as this is possible for man."[56] Now the divine, the ideal, the orderly is precisely what true fine art expresses. An epitome of Plato's teaching on this matter is contained in the following passage of the

[55] VI. 500c; cf. III. 395c-d. The above italicized formulation of the principle is that given by Alfred North Whitehead in one of his works.

[56] VI. 500c-d.

same dialogue: "Let our artists be those who are gifted to discern the true nature of the beautiful (*kalón*) and graceful (*eúschemon*); then our youth will dwell in a land of health amid fair sights and sounds, and receive the good in everything. And beauty, the effluence of fair works, shall flow into the eye and ear, like a health-giving breeze from a purer region, and insensibly draw the soul from the earliest years into a likeness (*homoiótes*) and concord (*symphonía*) with the beauty of reason."[57]

This Platonic principle, which we may call the *Principle of Assimilation*, is recognized by contemporary psychoanalysis. The latter calls it the Principle of *Identification*.[58] Psychoanalysis dwells on instances where the assimilation or identification is with what is negative, unhealthy. Thus, Anthony Storr, a British psychoanalyst, remarks, by way of example, that analysts themselves are exposed to identifying with, or becoming infected by, their

---

[57] III. 401c-d; cf. *Laws* II. 656, *Timaeus* 90d.

[58] Anthony Storr, *C.G. Jung*, New York,, 1973, p. 21.

patients. He notes that Jung "referred to analysts 'going queer,' and said that he thought Freud had been adversely affected by his patients."[59] Plato himself was keenly aware of the fact that the Principle of Assimilation operates in a negative as well as in a positive way. It was for this reason that he condemned pseudo art. Thus, he rejected the tragic poetry of his time because the heroes in this poetry provided wrong models for people, being depicted as overcome by sorrow, beating themselves hopelessly and wailing.[60]

Works of true art are viewed by Plato as working on the soul and improving it, not only by effecting an *assimilation* of the psyche to the ideals expressed by them, but also by way of *purification*.[61] The Greek word for purification is *catharsis*. The connotation of the term catharsis should not be confused with that of a contemporary school of psychology which employs it as a

[59] *Ibid.*

[60] See *Plato's Theory of Fine Art*, pp. 56-58.

[61] *Sophist* 226d.

synonym of *self-expression* in general. For Plato catharsis and the cognate term *catharmos* mean strictly purification, either of the body or of the psyche.[62] He defines purification as the removing of whatever is bad and the retaining of what is good.[63] In the case of the *body*, badness, which consists of deformity or disease, is removed by two means: by gymnastic, which removes deformity, and by the art and science of medicine, which removes disease.[64] In the case of the *psyche*, badness is removed by the fine arts, the sciences which we discussed earlier, and philosophy; in other words, by all those disciplines which Plato includes in the first division of education.

---

62 *Ibid.* 226d ff.; *Laws* I. 628d.

63 *Republic* VIII. 567c; *Sophist* 227d.

64 *Sophist* 228a ff.

6

THE ARTS AS THERAPY

a. Philosophy

There are various forms of badness or disease of the psyche. The chief of these, according to Plato, are ignorance, intemperance, injustice, and cowardice. As we have already seen, there are two kinds of ignorance: unconscious and conscious. Unconscious ignorance or intellectual conceit, the "large and grievous kind" of ignorance, as Plato calls it, is purged most effectively by means of *philosophy,*[65] particularly the use of dialectic in the form of the *élenchos*, that is, *cross-examination*, question-answer.[66] This method removes the conceit (*oíesis*) of knowledge, humbles one intellectually, making him realize what he knows

[65] *Phaedo* 82d.

[66] *Sophist* 229b ff.

and he does not know.[67] The elenchos "is the greatest and most efficacious of all purifications."[68]

To say that *philosophy*, or more precisely *a particular method of philosophy*, effects the *catharsis of unconscious ignorance* is not to assert that the fine arts can be of no use here. Plato's dialogues, in which the use of cross-examination is displayed in action, are outstanding works of art, are philosophical dramas, literary masterpieces. This is especially true of those dialogues in which Socrates is the dominant figure. Socrates was the greatest master of the *elenchos*, of cross-examination, known in history. And Plato, Socrates' most remarkable disciple, was the greatest master of philosophical dramas. He gave surpassing literary expression to the cross-examining that Socrates engaged in. As we read these philosophical dramas or dialogues, we find that *we ourselves* are undergoing examination, that *we ourselves* are be-

---

[67] *Ibid.* 230d.

[68] *Ibid.*

coming conscious of our ignorance and are being purged of intellectual pride. Here, then, is a most striking example of great art works that have the effect of purifying from the disease of unconscious ignorance.

In recent times, a comparable example are the 'aesthetic' works of the Danish philosopher Soren Kierkegaard, father of modern Existentialism. In his book *The Point of View for My Work as an Author*, Kierkegaard says he wrote his 'aesthetic' or 'literary' works for the purpose of effecting in his readers a spiritual transformation.

The other kind of ignorance, conscious ignorance, is purged away by instruction (*didaskaliké*) in those subjects in which one is ignorant.[69] Of course, one cannot study and master every branch of knowledge, every art and craft.[70] Plato shows the ridiculous situation of the itinerant teachers of his time known as Sophists, who

---

[69] *Ibid.* 229.

[70] *Ibid.* 233a.

claimed to be able to teach a great variety of subjects, some of them, such as Gorgias, going so far as to claim to be able to discuss any subject and to answer any question, by any one, at any time. Plato does not regard all conscious ignorance as evil, but only that which pertains to certain subjects, above all to the existence and nature of Deity, the nature and destiny of man, the nature of good and evil, the true scale of values, and the way of life that leads most effectively to man's highest fulfillment. With regard to the subject of God, it is to be noted that Plato characterizes *unbelief* in Deity, or a *wrong* conception of the Deity, as a disease (*nósos*).[71] Unbelief, the outright denial of the existence of God, is viewed by him as a disease that as a rule appears in the young and tends to disappear with the passage of time.[72] Some scientists in our time, such as Freud, regard religion, the belief in God, as an "obsessional neurosis,"

[71] *Laws* X. 888b.

[72] *Ibid*. 888b-c.

which one tends to outgrow.[73] Plato's view is evidently the *exact opposite* of this: it is atheism which is a neurosis, a disease, which one tends to outgrow. The Platonic view on this matter, it may be remarked, is by no means an antiquated one. It has been upheld in modern times by the famous English philosopher Francis Bacon, who says in one of his essays: "A little philosophy inclineth a man's mind to atheism; but depth in philosophy bringeth men's minds about to religion."[74] And in our time, the renowned Swiss psychologist to whom I have already made reference, Jung, who was nineteen years younger than Freud, held that a lively religious faith protects the individual from neurosis.[75]

Plato offers arguments to disprove two forms of atheism, that which says there is no God, and that which misconceives God, asserting for example that

---

[73] *The Future of an Illusion*, New York, Anchor Books, 1964, pp. 70-71.

[74] In his essay, *Of Atheism*.

[75] Anthony Storr, *op. cit.* p. 15.

Deity exercises no providence.[76] And as one very conscious of the power which literature has in this regard, he emphasizes the need of writers of narratives and poetry to speak truthfully about the divine. Thus, God's existence should be affirmed, and he should be depicted as perfect, all-good and all-wise, exercising providence for men, always causing good, never evil. When literature does this, Plato believes, it helps prevent the appearance of the disease of atheism or, if it has appeared, it helps cure it.[77]

b. Literature

With regard to the subject of *the destiny of man*, the Athenian philosopher again believes that literature can play a significant role in mental health. It is vitally important, he holds, that one have *true* ideas on this subject. He himself sought in his philosophical dramas to convey such ideas.

---

[76] *Republic* II. 377d-383c; *Laws* X. 885b ff.

[77] *Ibid.*

Thus, a large part of the *Phaedo* is devoted to the topic of the immortality of the human soul. Several other dialogues end with a lively treatment of the hereafter: the *Apology*, the *Gorgias*, and the *Republic*. Death is not the end of a man's life, he asserts, but only the separation of the real man, the soul, from the body. And the life of the soul after death is not less real than life on earth, with the body, but probably more real. That life is blissful for those who have attained goodness here, but painful for those who have led a life of wickedness. Plato emphasizes the need that *narrative writers and poets* express such ideas. False ideas on these matters, he remarks, "infect the soul with evil."[78] Cowardice is one such consequence;[79] for how can a man be courageous if he has fear of death, owing to false belief about it?[80] By conveying true ideas about God and man, good literature serves to remove ignorance and to prevent or cure the vice of

[78] *Phaedo* 115e; cf. *Republic* II. 381b.

[79] *Phaedo* 68d-e; *Republic* III. 386a-387c.

[80] *Republic* III. 386a-b.

cowardice, the harboring of unwarranted and weakening fear.

c. Comedy

Plato makes some noteworthy observations about the value of *comedy* in preventing and correcting another type of ignorance: self-ignorance. In the *Philebus*, discussing the *lucridous*, the *comic* (*to geloíon*), he asserts that in its main form it is that part of vice or baseness in general which consists in ignorance of oneself as an individual.[81] Self-ignorance involves a striking incongruity between what a man *is* and what he *thinks* he is. When noticed by others, it provokes in them laughter.[82] In Plato's dialogues, the incongruity usually exhibited is that between one's assumed knowledge and one's actual knowledge. Now to be in a state of delusion about oneself is, remarks our philosopher, an evil condition. The *elenchos* or method of cross-examination as employed by Socrates is viewed as a

81 48c-d.

82 49b.

potent means of freeing one of this particular form of unconscious ignorance. Comedy is another effective means. Provided it is not of the vulgar sort that resorts of obscenity, comedy helps us see ourselves as we really are, by exhibiting to us the ludicrous in others. By condemning the ludicrous through the laughter which it evokes in the audience, higher forms of comedy teach us *indirectly* to avoid doing and saying what is laughable, or developing faults which evoke laughter.[83] Since there are many such faults, it is necessary, Plato remarks, that comic performances always present some novel feature, display a different form of the ludicrous, and thus drive home a new point.[84]

d. Rhetoric

For the therapy of another form of disorder of the psyche that has been mentioned, *injustice*, Plato stresses the value of the *true* art of *rhetoric*. In the

---

[83] *Laws* VII. 816d-e.

[84] *Ibid.*

Gorgias, where Plato's main topic is the art of rhetoric, he discusses the relevance of this art to the therapy of injustice. Viewing injustice both as a state of the psyche and as an external act, he points out how rhetoric may be used for removing this vice and promoting the development of the excellence of justice in man. Thus, he remarks that the true rhetorician will always have before his mind "how injustice may be removed; how temperance may be bred in men and incontinence cut off; and how excellence as a whole may be produced and vice expelled."[85] *True rhetoric is the art of persuasion based on truth, on true knowledge of the subject which it treats and of ethical principles, and also of the psyche to which it addresses itself.* Plato presents Socrates as the greatest master of this art. And the dialogues of Plato are examples of true rhetoric, as he conceives it. In connection with the therapeutic nature of true rhetoric, it is worth noting that in the *Phaedrus*

---

[85] 504d-e.

rhetoric is compared with the art of medicine (*iatriké techne*). *Rhetoric is said to be to the soul what the art of medicine is to the body.* The one is concerned with therapy of the soul; the other, with the therapy of the body.[86] Thus, the true rhetorician is viewed as a *physician of the soul.* Having profound knowledge of the psyche, the art of rhetoric knows "what sort of man is influenced by what sort of speech and why,"[87] and accordingly uses in each case the most appropriate kind.

In the *Gorgias*, Plato particularly recommends the use of rhetoric to induce persons guilty of wrong-doing to *confess* their unjust acts. He recognizes that there is a tendency in men to *conceal* their guilt, to try to *deceive* themselves about their inner state of injustice, from which their wrong-doing sprang. Inner injustice is a disease (*nósema*),[88] which if not treated in time becomes incurable. A person who acts in this manner is like

---

[86] *Phaedrus* 270b; cf. *Protagoras* 313e.

[87] *Phaedrus* 271e.

[88] *Gorgias* 480b; cf. *Sophist* 228d.

one who is suffering from a serious bodily illness and hides it from everyone, instead of hastening to a physician to be examined and treated by all necessary means.[89] It is to the vital interest of the wrong-doer to hasten to the judge, confess his unjust act, and ask to pay the penalty. For by exposing his injustice and accepting the penalty the soul is cured of the disease. In cases where persons do not do this, some possessor of the art of true rhetoric, says Plato, ought to use his art. He should approach such a person, whether it be one of his relatives or some friend, and persuade him "to bring his iniquity to light, in order that he may pay the penalty and be made healthy."[90] He should instill courage in such a person, persuading him not to be afraid of doing this and of accepting without

---

[89] *Gorgias* 479a-b; cf. *Republic* IX. 591: "What shall he profit, if his injustice be undetected and unpunished? He who is undetected only gets worse, whereas he who is detected and punished has the brutal part of his nature silenced and humanized, and the gentler element is liberated and his whole soul is perfected and enobled by the acquirement of justice...."

[90] *Ibid.* 480b-c.

resentment whatever punishment is deemed proper. The punishment may be a fine, it may be a flogging, it may be imprisonment, it may be exile, it may even be death.[91] It will vary according to the nature of the act, just as medical treatment for the body varies, sometimes calling for a purgative, sometimes for cauterization, and sometimes for cutting.[92]

Plato's viewpoint in this matter was shared by the great Russian novelist Fyodor Dostoievsky. In *The Brothers Karamazov*, Dmitri Karamazov expresses the conviction that only through punishment will he be purified, and hence ungrudgingly accepts the punishment inflicted upon him for a murder he did not actually commit. Although Dmitri Karamazov did not kill his father, as he was accused of having done, still he confesses: "I meant to kill him, and perhaps I really might have killed him." The punishment, he believes, will serve to ease his

---

[91] *Ibid.* 480d.

[92] *Ibid.* 480c.

conscience for having harbored such evil thoughts, and will cleanse the inner man. He says: "I accept the torture of accusation, and my public shame, and want to suffer because by suffering I shall be purified."[93] Dostoievsky analyzes the inner dimension of punishment, and thus helps us understand how punishment effects the cure of such a disease of the soul.

True rhetoric, the art of persuasive eloquent speech, spoken or written, based on a profound understanding of the human psyche and guided by sound ethical principles, succeeds in initiating the process of therapy of the psyche by leading the guilty person to *confession*, to *self-blame* and to the *ungrudging acceptance of punishment.* True rhetoric avoids the use of invective, of angry denunciation or accusation as an ineffective approach to the psyche. It seeks, instead, to persuade

---

93 *The Brothers Karamazov*, trans. by Constance Garnett, New York, The Modern Library, 1950, p. 618.

by means of reasoning and the use of gentle and beautiful speech.[94]

e. Music

In connection with the therapy of *cowardice* and *intemperance*, Plato especially calls attention to the value of *music*, in the narrower sense of this term, and of the dance. The ancient Greeks seldom used what we call 'pure music,' i.e., music without words. They generally used *music* in conjunction with *words*, *poetry*. So when Plato speaks of 'music' in the narrower sense of the term, he means *song*, with or without instrumental accompaniment. True poetry not only conveys sound ideas on vital matters, but also possesses elements of rhythm and harmony kindred to music.[95] The power which music in this sense has upon the soul, Plato believes, is unsurpassed by any other agency, so far as the formation of moral character is concerned. "For rhythm and harmony find their way into the

---

[94] Cf. *Laws* X. 887c-888a; *Phaedrus* 271c ff.

[95] *Republic* VII. 522a.

inward places of the soul, on which they mightily fasten, imparting grace and making the soul of him who is rightly educated graceful."[96] This means that through rhythm and harmony music affects the psyche at the level of consciousness, as well as at the level of subconsciousness, and does so in a powerful manner and with lasting effects.

For preventing cowardice, curing it, and developing courage, Plato recommends the use of the *Dorian* Mode of music. This mode "fittingly imitates the utterances and the accents of a brave man who is engaged in warfare or in any other hard and dangerous task, and who acts with firm step and a determination to endure."[97] Certain other modes, notably the *Ionian* and the *Lydian*, the *Mixolydian* and the *Hypolydian*, are viewed as quite unsuitable for this purpose, as tending to weaken moral fiber instead of strengthening it. They are 'slack' and hence tend to instill softness, weakness. For

---

[96] *Ibid.* III. 401d-e; cf. *Laws* VII. 812b-c.

[97] *Republic* III. 399a.

developing temperance, for preventing and curing intemperance, Plato recommends the use of the *Phrygian* Mode. This mode expresses "peaceful action under no stress of hard necessity, as when a man is using persuasion or entreaty, praying to the gods, or instructing and admonishing his neighbor, exhibiting wise restraint and contentment."[98]

These views are presented in the *Republic*. They reappear in the *Laws* in substantially the same form. In the *Republic*, Plato stresses the need of employing certain musical modes and avoiding others, and also of employing simple rhythms and avoiding the use of many instruments. "For complexity in music engenders intemperance," just as in regimen it engenders bodily disease; whereas simplicity in music engenders temperance in the soul, and in regimen health of body.[99]

The value of music in treating intemperance and cultivating temperance is noted also in the

---

[98] *Ibid.*

[99] *Ibid.* III. 404e.

Charmides. Recommended for this purpose are certain songs, denoted by the word *epodaí*. This is a term that often appears in Plato's dialogues. It is rendered by English translators as 'incantations,' 'charms,' and 'chant.' In the *Charmides*, these songs are said to consist of beautiful words,[100] but nothing is said about their content. From other writings of Plato, especially the *Laws*, we learn that they are poetic compositions set to music, and designed to attract the young to virtue, and to this end should be repeated as often as possible.[101]

Plato sums up the therapeutic function of music when he says: "Music was granted to us for the sake of harmony; the harmony of music is meant to correct any discord which may have arisen in the courses of the soul, and to be our ally in bringing her into harmony and agreement with herself; and the rhythm of music was meant to be a helper for the same ends.[102] And again, when he says: "Music

---

[100] *Charmides* 157a.

[101] *Laws* II. 665c, 670e, 671a; cf. *Phaedo* 77e-78a.

[102] *Timaeus* 47c-d; cf. *Laws* II. 659e.

by harmony makes men harmonious, and by rhythm rhythmical."[103]

f. The Dance

The relevance of the dance to *courage* and *temperance*, and to the opposites of these, is discussed in the *Laws*. As we have seen, Plato set the dance apart from the other fine arts, placing it in the second major division of education: gymnastic. The dance is a form of physical exercise, and its direct aim is to make the *body* healthy and strong, beautiful and agile, whereas the other fine arts, which belong to the first division of education, have as their object the improvement of the soul. The dance is *somatotherapeutic*, concerned with the improvement of the *soma*, the body, whereas the other arts are *psychotherapeutic*, concerned with the improvement of the psyche, and of the body through the psyche. However, as has already been pointed out, although the direct aim of gymnastic is the care

---

[103] *Republic* VII. 522a.

and improvement of the body, it also has beneficent effects on the soul. The true or noble forms of the dance improve the condition of the body, making it an efficient instrument of the soul, and in addition are conductive to the improvement of the soul, through harmonious postures and rhythmic bodily movements.[104] War dances, which imitate the postures and movements of those engaged courageously in war and vehement action tend, on Platonic principles, to remove cowardice and foster the development of courage, while dances of peace, which exhibit a temperate soul in the enjoyment of prosperity and modest pleasures, tend to purify one of intemperance and to promote the development of temperance.

There is implicit in Plato's teaching here a principle of wider import than the James-Lange Theory of Emotions. According to the James-Lange theory, emotion follows the attendant physiological changes. Plato would have remarked that this is half

---

[104] *Laws* II. 672e.

the truth: the whole truth is that emotion sometimes follows physiological changes, being occasioned by them, and at other times *precedes* them, causing such changes. And he would have added that the James-Lange theory says nothing about the important relationship between bodily *postures* and *gestures* on the one hand, and settled dispositions (*héxeis*) of the soul—traditionally known as *virtues* and *vices*—on the other. It is Plato's view that states of the soul, such as courage and temperance, find expression in certain bodily attitudes and gestures, and conversely, that such bodily attitudes and gestures tend to dispose one to courage and temperance.[105] Because of his deep realization of this, Plato emphasized the need of selecting certain postures and movements for the dances and excluding others. And further, he suggested that painters could play a valuable role in depicting the right postures and movements, those expressive of

---

[105] See *Laws* II. 655 ff.

beauty, particularly of the beauty of temperance and courage.[106]

With regard to temperance and intemperance, I must add to what I have said thus far that Plato assigns great importance to temperance as a factor in physical health, and to intemperance as a factor in physical disease. In the *Charmides*, where he sets forth briefly his theory of psychosomatic therapy, young Charmides is said to have been suffering from headaches. Socrates advises him to strive to acquire the virtue of temperance, and remarks: "When temperance is *engendered* in our souls, and present, we may easily secure health to the head and the rest of the body also.[107] When, on the other hand, intemperance is present, multiform maladies arise in the body. Plato points this out particularly in the *Timaeus*. He remarks that if the rational faculty does not observe measure in its activity, if it does not allow enough time for exercise and rest of the

---

[106] *Laws* II. 656d-e.

[107] *Charmides* 157a.

body, it will end up by shattering the health of the body. "Whenever," he says, "the soul over eagerly pursues some study or investigation, it wastes the body."[108] Similarly, when the spirited element does not restrain its tendency to controversy and contention, which arises from its striving for glory and power, the health of the body is ruined. "When the soul engages in teachings and battles of words carried on with controversy and contention," he observes, "it makes the body inflamed and shakes it to pieces."[109] Finally, when moderation is not exercised with respect to the appetites, and there is, for instance, excessive eating, there result many bodily illnesses.[110]

g. Other Arts

I have discussed the therapeutic role which can be played by fine art in the form of philosophical

---

[108] *Timaeus* 88a.

[109] *Ibid.*

[110] *Ibid.* 72e; cf. *Republic* III. 408a-b.

dramas, *narratives*, *poetry*, *comedy*, *rhetoric*, *music* and the *dance*. I will add now a few words about three other arts that Plato occasionally mentions in his works: *architecture*, *painting*, and *sculpture*. He does not go into special discussions as regards the effects each of these arts has on the psyche. Evidently he does not think that their influence is as strong as that of the other arts that I have mentioned and discussed. However, it is clear that he does not consider their influence as negligible. In the *Republic* he makes the general observation that when they are expressive of the ideal, of beauty, of harmony, these arts exercise a healthful influence upon the psyche, in accordance with the principle that we become like that which we habitually contemplate.

7

CONCLUDING REMARKS

In view of the many things that Plato says about the prevention and therapy of diseases of the psyche and the body by means of the fine arts, philosophy, exercise and regimen, one may wonder whether he assigned any value to other means, particularly surgery and medicines. The answer is that he does recognize the need of surgery in certain cases—the need of "cutting and burning," as he calls it. This is implicit in a remark of his that was quoted earlier in connection with the treatment of injustice. As far as medicines are concerned, he recommends the avoidance of them as far as possible. Characteristic in this regard is his observation that whenever anyone does violence to a malady by drugging, "diseases many and grave, in place of few and slight, are wont to occur."[111] There is only one

[111] *Timaeus* 89c-d.

'medicine' (*phármakon*) that Plato considers truly excellent and recommends to all: wisdom.[112] This view is quite in accord with the following statement of Hippocrates, the Father of the medical art: "Between wisdom and the medical art there is no gulf fixed. In fact, the medical art possesses all the qualities that make for wisdom."[113]

I will end this lecture by making two more brief remarks. Firstly, it is evident from this presentation of Plato's teaching on the relevance of the fine arts to therapy that this teaching is many-sided and profound, and certainly applicable in our time. Secondly, it should be realized that the methods which Plato advocates for the therapy of body and soul, in particular the functions which he assigns to the fine arts, are not mere speculations, untested personal theories. They are methods that had been conceived and applied in Greece long before his time. The guild of Greek physicians known as the

---

[112] *Critias* 89c-d; cf. *Republic* X. 595b.

[113] Hippocrates, *On Decorum*, in Loeb Classical Library, *Hippocrates*, Vo. II, p. 287.

descendants of Asklepios (or Aesculapius) used poetry and music for the treatment of physical and mental disorders.[114] And there are in Plato's dialogues references to Asklepios and the Asklepiads, and expressions of admiration for them. Also, there is ample evidence that the famous pre-Socratic philosopher Pythagoras and his followers used these arts for the therapy of the body and the psyche.[115]

Plato himself praises Pythagoras highly in the tenth book of the *Republic*, for having handed down to posterity a Pythagorean "way of life" (*trópos tou bíou*).[116] The originality of Plato lies in the fact that he pointed out the relevance of *all* the fine arts to therapy, and also in the fact that he grounded this

---

[114] P. Kabbadias, *To Hierón tou Asklepioú en Epidaúro kai he Therapeía ton Asthenón ("The Sanctuary of Asklepios at Epidaurus and the Therapy of the Sick")*, Athens, 1900, pp. 288-289; Emma J. Edelstein and Ludwig Edelstein, *Asclepius*, Baltimore, 1945, Vol. II, pp. 119-208.

[115] See e.g., my book *Pythagoras on the Fine Arts of Therapy*, Belmont, Massachusetts, 1994.

[116] *Republic* X. 600b.

relevance in his total philosophy: in his theory of man, in his psychology, in his theory of education, in his aesthetics and ethics, and in his general theory of reality.

A GREEK SUMMARY
BY DR. M. DRAGONA-MONACHOU

Στὸ ἄρθρο αὐτὸ ὁ συγγραφεὺς συζητᾶ τὶς ἀπόψεις τοῦ Πλάτωνος γιὰ τὸ ρόλο ποὺ μποροῦν νὰ παίξουν οἱ καλὲς τέχνες στὴ θεραπεία ἀσθενειῶν καὶ εὐρύτερα στὴ βελτίωση τῆς ψυχοσωματικῆς κατάστασης τοῦ ἀνθρώπου. Παρὰ τὸ γεγονὸς ὅτι ἡ πλατωνικὴ διδασκαλία δὲν ἀναπτύσσεται σὲ ἕνα συγκεκριμένο ἔργο, ἀλλὰ εἶναι ἐγκατεσπαρμένη σὲ πολλοὺς διαλόγους, μὲ κέντρο ὡστόσο τὴν *Πολιτεία* καὶ τοὺς *Νόμους*, ὁ συγγραφεὺς τὴ θεωρεῖ πλουσιώτατη καὶ πολύτιμη. Καὶ δὲν βρίσκει νὰ ἔχη διευρυνθῇ ἱκανοποιητικά.

Ὅπως εἶναι φυσικό, σὲ μεγάλη ἔκταση συζητεῖται ἡ πλατωνικὴ θεωρία τοῦ ἀνθρώπου, ἡ σχέση σώματος καὶ ψυχῆς καὶ κυρίως ἡ δομὴ τῆς ψυχῆς καὶ οἱ ἀρετὲς τῶν μερῶν-δυνάμεών της. Δίνεται ἰδιαίτερη ἔμφαση στὴν ψυχή, καὶ γιατὶ ὡς κινητική, δυναμική, δημιουργικὴ καὶ μορφοποιητικὴ ἀρχὴ ἐξουσιάζει τὸ σῶμα—καὶ ὁ ρόλος τοῦ ἀσύνειδου μέρους της εἶναι σημαντικὸς γιὰ τὸν ἀναβολισμό του—ἀλλὰ καί γιατὶ οἱ νόσοι τοῦ ἀνθρώπου ὡς ψυχοσωματικῆς ὁλότητας προέρχονται ἀπὸ τὴ διασάλευση τῆς ἱεραρχίας τῶν δυνάμεων τῆς ψυχῆς, ὅπως ἀντίθετα ἀπὸ τὴν ἐναρμόνισή τους ἐξαρτᾶται ἡ ὑγεία του. Ψυχικὰ νοσήματα εἶναι ἡ ἄγνοια (κυρίως ἡ ἀμάθεια), ἡ ἀκρασία, ἡ δειλία καὶ ἡ ἀδικία, μὲ συνέπεια τὴν ἀσθένεια, τὴν ἀσχήμια καὶ τὴν ἀδυναμία τῆς ψυχῆς καὶ κυρίως τὴν ἐνθρόνιση στὴ θέση τοῦ ἡγεμονικοῦ παρανόμων ἐπιθυμιῶν, ὅπως αὐτὲς ποὺ ἐκδηλώνονται στὸν ὕπνο χωρὶς στὸ ξύπνιο νὰ μποροῦν νὰ ἐλεγχθοῦν· γενικώτερα ἡ ἄνοια καὶ ἡ μανία, στὴν παθολογικὴ καὶ ὄχι στὴν παραφυσιολογικὴ ἤ ὑπερ-φυσιολογική της μορφὴ τῆς ἱερᾶς μανίας.

Αἰτιακοὶ παράγοντες τῶν καταστάσεων αὐτῶν, ποὺ ἀντιστοιχοῦν στὶς νεώτερες παράνοια καὶ σχιζοφρένεια, εἶναι ἡ δυσαρμονία, ἡ ἀταξία, ἡ ἀσυμφωνία καὶ γενικὰ ἡ ἔλλειψη ρυθμοῦ. Γιὰ τοῦτο καὶ παντοδύναμος καὶ ἀποφασιστικὸς εἶναι ὁ ρόλος τῶν καλῶν τεχνῶν καὶ προληπτικὰ καὶ θεραπευτικά, δηλ. καὶ γιὰ τὴν ἁρμονικὴ ἀνάπτυξη τοῦ ἀνθρώπου καὶ γιὰ τὴν καταπολέμηση τῆς διασάλευσης τῆς σωστῆς τάξης. Πρωταρχικώτερα εἶναι βέβαια τὰ πνευματικὰ μέσα· γιὰ τοῦτο καὶ ἡ προτεραιότητα ποὺ δίνεται στὴ μουσικὴ ἀπὸ τὴ γυμναστικὴ στὸ πλατωνικὸ πρόγραμμα τῆς ὀρθῆς παιδείας.

Ἡ "μουσικὴ" περιλαμβάνει γενικῶς τὶς τέχνες καὶ εἰδικώτερα τὶς καλὲς τέχνες (μουσική, ζωγραφική, γλυπτική, λογοτεχνία), τὰ μαθηματκά, τὴν ἀστρονομία, τὴν ἁρμονική, τὴ φιλοσοφία τῆς ἐπιστήμης καὶ τὴ φιλοσοφία, τὸν ἀνώτατο κλάδο τῶν ἐπιστημῶν. Ἡ "μουσικὴ" φροντίζει γιὰ τὴν ἁρμονικὴ ἀνάπτυξη τῆς ψυχῆς καὶ τὴν κάθαρσή της ἀπὸ ἐλαττώματα καὶ κακίες. Ζητᾶ ὄχι μόνο νὰ ἀναπτύξη σωστὰ τὶς δυνατότητες τῆς ψυχῆς, ἀλλὰ καὶ νὰ θεραπεύσῃ καταστάσεις ἀρρώστιας, ὅταν ἔχουν ἤδη ἀναπτυχθῇ. Ἀπὸ τὴ γυμναστική, παράλληλα μὲ τὴ δίαιτα καὶ τὴν ἄσκηση, μεγάλη εἶναι ἡ σημασία τοῦ χοροῦ γιὰ τὸ παθητικὸ μέρος τῆς ψυχῆς.

Μόνο βέβαια οἱ ἀληθινὲς τέχνες καὶ ὄχι οἱ ψευδοτέχνες εἶναι ἀποτελεσματικὰ μέσα ψυχοθεραπείας καὶ ἔχουν ἀξία ὡς μέσα παιδευτικά. Ἡ παιδευτική τους ἀποτελεσματικότητα δὲν περιορίζεται στὴ θέση ποὺ πρέπει νὰ ἔχουν στὴν ἐκπαίδευση, ἀλλὰ ἐπεκτείνεται σὲ ὅλα τὰ στάδια τῆς ἀνθρώπινης παιδείας μὲ τὴν πολιτιστικὴ ἐπίδραση ποὺ ἀσκοῦν. Ἔτσι ἡ ἀρχιτεκτονική, ἡ ζωγραφικὴ καὶ ἡ γλυπτική, ἐμπνεόμενες ἀπὸ ἰδεώδη καὶ ἐμπνέοντας ἰδεώδη, ἐπιδροῦν εὐεργετικὰ ἀπὸ τὴ θέση τους στὰ πλαίσια τῆς κοινότητας καὶ στὸ περιβάλλον. Οἱ λοιπὲς τέχνες ἐπενεργοῦν καὶ ἀκαδημαϊκά, ἀλλὰ καὶ μὲ τὴν παρουσία τους σ' ὅλες τὶς ἐκδηλώσεις τῆς ζωῆς.

Ἐπιτομὴ τῆς πλατωνικῆς διδασκαλίας γιὰ

τὴν ἐπίδραση τῶν ἀληθινῶν καλῶν τεχνῶν στὸν ἄνθρωπο θεωρεῖ ὁ συγγραφέας τὸ χωρίο 401 c-d τῆς *Πολιτείας*, στὸ ὁποῖο ἐπισημαίνεται ἡ ἀνάγκη τῆς ἀποδοχῆς τῶν "δημιουργῶν" ἐκείνων ποὺ ἡ τέχνη τους μιμεῖται τὰ θεῖα, τὰ ἰδεώδη καὶ τὰ εὔτακτα.

Ἡ πλατωνικὴ ἀρχή, ποὺ μπορεῖ νὰ ὀνομασθῆ "ἀρχὴ τῆς ἀφομοίωσης", ἀναγνωρίζεται—ἀρνητικὰ—ἀπὸ τὴ σύγχρονη ψυχολογία ὡς ἀρχὴ τῆς "ταύτισης". Ἀλλὰ οἱ καλὲς τέχνες δὲν ἐπενεργοῦν μόνο ἀφομοιωτικὰ στὴν ψυχή, ἀλλὰ καὶ καθαρτικά, ἀπομακρύνοντας δηλ. τὴ δυσαρμονία, τὴν κακία καὶ τὴν ἀκρασία καὶ κρατῶντας μόνο ὅ,τι εἶναι ἀγαθό. Εἰδικώτερα ἡ ἀμάθεια καθαίρεται ἀπὸ τὴ φιλοσοφία, κυρίως τὴ διαλεκτικὴ καὶ τὸν ἔλεγχο, καὶ ἡ ἄγνοια στὰ ὁριακὰ προβλήματα ἀπὸ τὴ σωστὴ διδασκαλία. Πρόσφορα μέσα παρέχει ἀκόμη ἡ λογοτεχνία καὶ μάλιστα ἡ κωμωδία καὶ ἡ ἀγαθὴ ρητορικὴ γιὰ τὴ θεραπεία ἰδιαίτερα τῆς ἔλλειψης αὐτογνωσίας καὶ τῆς ἀδικίας. Ἡ ποινὴ ἀποτελεῖ τὴν ἀποτελεσματικώτερη κάθαρση τῆς ἀδικίας. Καὶ ὁ ἀνδροπρεπὴς χορὸς καὶ ἡ μουσική εἶναι ἀπαράμιλλα γιὰ τὴ θεραπεία τῆς δειλίας καὶ τῆς ἀκρασίας καὶ τὴ διαμόρφωση τοῦ ἠθικοῦ χαρακτῆρα. Γιατὶ ἐπιδροῦν καὶ στὸ ὑποσυνείδητο. Ὑπονοεῖται καὶ στὸν Πλάτωνα μὲ εὐρύτερη ἔννοια ἡ ἀρχὴ τῆς θεωρίας τῶν συναισθημάτων τῶν James-Lange.

Ὁ συγγραφεὺς πιστεύει συμπερασματικὰ ὅτι ἡ πολύπλευρη καὶ βαθειὰ διδασκαλία τοῦ Πλάτωνος ἔχει τὴ θέση της στὴν ἐποχή μας. Καὶ δὲν πρόκειται γιὰ μιὰ ἁπλῆ θεωρία, ἀλλὰ γιὰ μιὰ γνώση ποὺ συνειδητοποιήθηκε καὶ ἐφαρμόσθηκε στὴν Ἑλλάδα, πολὺ πρὶν ἀπὸ τὸ καιρό του ἀπὸ τοὺς Ἀσκληπιάδες καὶ τοὺς Πυθαγορείους. Ὁ Πλάτων ὅμως τόνισε τὴ σχέση ὅλων τῶν καλῶν τεχνῶν μὲ τὴ ψυχοθεραπεία καὶ θεμελίωσε τὴ σχέση αὐτὴ σ᾽ ὅλη του τὴ φιλοσοφία: στὴ θεωρία του γιὰ τὸν ἄνθρωπο, στὴν ψυχολογία του, στὴ θεωρία τῆς παιδείας, στὴν αἰσθητική, τὴν ἠθικὴ καὶ τὴ γενικὴ του θεωρία τῆς πραγματικότητας.

DIALOGUES OF PLATO REFERRED TO

INDEX OF PROPER NAMES

INDEX OF SUBJECTS

COMMENTS ON A RELATED WORK

PYTHAGORAS ON THE FINE ARTS AS THERAPY

In his book *Pythagoras and the Fine Arts as Therapy*, the eminent writer of noteworthy philosophical works Constantine Cavarnos discusses Pythagoras' views on the therapeutic action of the fine arts on the health of the body and the psyche, a subject which he was invited to lecture on at Wellesley College in Massachusetts.

The book has three chapters. In the first chapter he presents the life of Pythagoras and his philosophical system. Pythagoras was one of the world's greatest men, according to John Burnet, eminent English historian of ancient Greek philosophy. He was admired and honored by the ancients, and had established a school which had followers over a period of many centuries, called "Pythagoreans." His ideas had given direction and orientation to all the Pre-Socratic philosophers and to Plato.

In the second chapter he develops the Pythagorean conception of the universe as a harmonious "cosmos," which means an orderly system. In his comprehensive conception of the world, Pythagoras related "form" to numbers, harmony, the beautiful, symmetry, and their influence on the body and the soul of man.

In the third chapter is explained the therapeutic influence of harmony in the form of music, poetry, and the dance on the soul and the body, as is testified to in the writings of various interpreters of Pythagoras. The most noted of those cited here are Aristoxenos, Plato, Aristotle, and the Neo-Platonists Porphyry and Iamblichos. Melody, poetry, and the dance restore the equilibrium of the soul and purify it of the passions, such as sorrow, as is pointed out in passages of the interpreters of Pythagoras' system just mentioned. For Pythagoras the fine arts were means or preserving and restoring order in the psyche and the body.

There follow three Appendixes which present testimonies on the therapeutic influence of music and poetry in the writings of ancient and Byzantine authors, and in addition in the works of the contemporary Greek musicologist Simon Karas. The latter says that the chief gift of God to man is *speech* (*logos*), which when united with rhythm becomes *poetry*, and when combined with melody becomes *music*, and when combined with movement becomes *dance*. These arts, when they were accompanied by suitable musical instruments —the cithara or the lyre—for religious hymns and heroic songs, inspired devoutness, seriousness, simplicity, frugality, and dignity.

With his many-sided culture and philosophical thought, Cavarnos has very skillfully gathered in this book a treasure of excellent teachings contained in the unique creations of the classical writers of Antiquity.

Panagiotis K. Georgountzos,
in *Platon*, Vol. 46, Athens, 1994.

In *Pythagoras and the Fine Arts as Therapy*, Dr. Cavarnos writes of Pythagoras' belief that beauty, as expressed in the Fine Arts, helps to purify the soul, "making it harmonious, good, and beautiful," and that the contemplation of beautiful works of art is extremely helpful as well in restoring the body to health. This is most remarkedly the case with music, an art form that particularly, and in the most direct fashion, touches the very wellsprings of human emotions. Since the functioning of the body is directly controlled by the mind, a healthy mind is seen as contributing to a healthy body.

Much of modern science, especially psychology, tends to confirm these theories. It is known, for example, that countless debilitating diseases of the body have psychosomatic origins.

The significance for us moderns is that so many contemporary cultural works, to a large degree, are inharmonious, in fact are intentionally dissonant, raucous, and coarse. Much modern music, poetry, literature, painting, and sculpture seem in their calculated ugliness to emanate from some fountainhead of bedlam, or even of hell itself. Could this be some constituent element in a process of deliberate cultural debasement? It would seem entirely possible, and the particular value of this penetrating essay by Dr. Cavarnos is that it provides one the keys to comprehending this process and, most saliently, to formulating a remedy.

James Thorton, in *The New American*,
February 3, 1997